Investin Etherum Cryptocurrencies & Profiting Guide

Table of Contents

Introduction

10 years ago, digital currency was almost unheard of except in small, elite circles. Today, all we hear are words like "cryptocurrency," "Bitcoin," "Blockchain" and now new ones, "Ethereum" and "smart contracts." All these words and more are fast becoming part of everyday language, no matter where you are in the world and, while most people now have a better understanding of them, especially Bitcoin, Ethereum remains something of a mystery to most people.

Ethereum is the world's first platform that will allow us to run applications in a way that is trustless, uncensorable and unstoppable – the three qualities that make cryptocurrencies so popular. All three of these qualities can be taken and applied to just about any application you could possibly think of. Smart contracts are the future of the world as we know it, contracts that will run automatically without the need for intermediaries and without the need for worry about whether they can be fulfilled or not.

Bitcoin started slowly and built up a head of steam that just keeps on billowing out and many people believe that Ethereum is just the next Bitcoin. It isn't; it is so much more than that. Ethereum is the future, second to Bitcoin only in terms of the volumes of transactions carried out on it. It has grown exponentially faster than Bitcoin in a much shorter period and some of that may be attributed to Bitcoin boosting confidence and excitement levels in digital currencies, but Ethereum stands apart from all the others.

Bitcoin was complicated; you needed to have an understanding of cryptography and a lot of disposable income that you could spend on the equipment needed to mine it. Ethereum changes all that and makes using the blockchain easy, putting it in within reach of Joe Public. It gives more people more chances to make more money.

It's time to learn what Ethereum can do for you and how it's more than just a blockchain currency. Ethereum is the Queen to the Bitcoin King; the Silver to the Bitcoin Gold but it has the potential to take the crown in both. Ethereum is a digital asset, one that could be one of the greatest investments you have ever made. Indeed, Ethereum is better suited to investment than Bitcoin ever was, simply because it is easier to make money with it without spending a fortune on it.

In this guide, you will learn:

- What Ethereum is
- How it works
- What Smart Contracts are
- All about Ethereum mining
- How to invest in Ethereum
- How it is used already in the world today
- Where it is heading in the future

You may be surprised to learn that there are already dozens of major organizations that use Ethereum and smart contracts. You may be even more surprised to learn that investing in

Ethereum is not difficult and anyone can do it – I will show you how to do it - although, as with any investment - you do need to understand that there is a risk involved. That's the nature of investing and, as long as you understand that from the beginning, there is no reason why you can't make some serious money.

Right now, the price of Ethereum is rising fast and it is now one of the most promising and most sought-after cryptocurrencies in the world. Want to learn more? Read on to discover everything you need to know about Ethereum.

Chapter 1: What is Ethereum?

If you have been following the financial news or the tech news, no doubt you have seen and heard the word "Ethereum." Normally, you will have heard it in connection with Bitcoin but the two are not be confused. Ethereum is one of the fastest growing cryptocurrencies in the world but, strictly speaking, Ethereum isn't a cryptocurrency as such.

It is actually a platform that lets developers build decentralize applications, conduct transactions and draw up smart contracts. This is all done with a currency known as Ether, another form of the cryptocurrency that does not have a physical form and is created entirely through encryption. It is nothing more than data on a digital ledger, a ledger that we all know of as the blockchain. This blockchain is shared far and wide publicly, on every computer that has the right software on it. Whenever a transaction takes place, it is added to a block and that block is validated by some of the computers on the network. The most crucial part of this, the part that ensures transactions cannot be tampered with, is that the ledger is shared in its entirety, every time a new transaction happens, with all network computers, or nodes as they are called. Anyone can see this ledger and can track every single Ethereum transaction that has ever happened – if anyone tried to make any changes, everyone would be able to see it.

The transactions are validated by miners and this is done through the solving of highly complex mathematical equations. I will be talking more about mining in a later chapter but, suffice to say, for now, it is intensive. The miners are rewarded for validating the blocks with a payment of a certain amount of Ether.

When a transaction is carried out using a cryptocurrency, the transaction is authenticated by a digital signature. This is created through two cryptography keys. The first is a public key, which is your Ethereum "address" and, whenever you are sent Ether, it is sent to that address. When you send Ether to someone else, a private key is used. This is a kind of password, randomly generated, that gives you the authority to carry out a transaction with the Ether, generating a message that creates the digital signature. This signature is then used by the miners to verify the transaction. Each new transaction has a unique signature, generated each time, stopping transactions from being repeated.

Why is this so important?

In the past, digital transactions have always needed a third-party like a bank, to authorize that transaction and validate it. Digital money is, at its most basic, a file which

may be copied and then reused but these intermediaries are not free – every bank and every authority requires everyone else to pay the fees they demand for letting them play in their sandbox.

The idea behind cryptocurrencies is to get around these authorities but transactions still need to be tracked to stop double-spending. Let's face it, if anyone could just go and create a copy of the digital currency they hold, and keep on spending it over and over, the currency would become next to useless.

The blockchain allows P2P (peer to peer) transactions without the need for that third party. They are secure by nature because nothing can be tampered with or changed without everybody on the network seeing it and having to revalidate the transaction.

All of this applies to Ethereum in the same way that it does to Bitcoin but both have completely different goals. Bitcoin is ONLY a digital currency, designed as a way of making payment for a service or goods, whereas Ethereum goes much further – it is a platform that allows the use of tokens to create applications, run them and, perhaps, more importantly, the ability to create smart contracts.

What is a smart contract?

A smart contract is a piece of code that will run when conditions that are specifically defined are met. The uses of a smart contract are virtually limitless, especially where the result required is exchange. Many companies are now using these smart contracts in the supply chain to ensure the quality of their products and the dispatch of them.

A smart contract is a contract that has been written in computer code and uploaded by the creator to the blockchain. Whenever a contract is executed, every computer on the network runs it because it is stored on the blockchain and is, in theory, tamper-proof.

If you understand computer programming, you will understand me when I say that a smart contract is a structured if...then statement. Provided specific conditions are met, the terms of the contract will be carried out. An example would be if you wanted to rent a vehicle and the company uses Ethereum. A smart contract would be drawn up and generated – the condition would be that you send a specified amount of funds. When that is met, a digital key is sent to you so that you can unlock the car.

This is all done on the blockchain so that when the Ether tokens are sent the whole network sees what has happened. In the same way, that network can also see that the key has been sent to you. Another condition could be added to this contract - one that says if the key is not sent to you then your tokens will be refunded. This transaction cannot be tampered with because everyone can see it.

Each program that is on Ethereum needs to use a certain amount of processing power and because this is all run by the network nodes, superfluous activities need to be kept to an absolute minimum. Because of this, every program and every contract on Ethereum is provided with a cost of gas. This is a measurement of the amount of processing power needed for the contract or program – the higher the requirement in gas, the more it will cost the user in Ether tokens.

The smart contract effectively removes the need for intermediaries like banks, notaries or lawyers which mean no fees to pay and this is important for those who reside in countries where the legal system is inefficient or downright corrupt. One downside to this is that if something went wrong such as a bug in the coding, the contract terms would still be carried out and this could cause problems.

That said, things are improving all the time and work on Ethereum is ongoing. It is still one of the safest ways to carry out a transaction and set up a contract.

Chapter 2: Ethereum vs Bitcoin vs Litecoin

There is no doubt that Bitcoin remains the largest cryptocurrency in the world but Ethereum is snapping hard at its heels. While the two do function similarly, they are designed and structured in very different ways. Where Bitcoin is a blockchain-based currency, allowing for the safe and anonymous transfer of funds with no regulation or centralized authority, Ethereum has borrowed the blockchain but expanded it for much more than just a payment method.

Currency vs Computer

The blockchain technology needs a very large distributed network to function, a transaction ledger where every single transaction gets recorded on every point of the network. This gives users the ability to send and receive the currency without a bank overseeing every move they make and charging well for the privilege.

Ethereum and Bitcoin are both based on this blockchain but Ethereum can do so much more and can accept much more advanced commands. This is because it has added a Turing-complete language to all interactions on the blockchain. This is what enables the smart contracts to be created. You could say that Ethereum is a virtual computer, built out of nodes on the blockchain and with each command having to be confirmed by the whole computer and saved to the ledger.

Bitcoin blocks hold transaction information but Ethereum blocks hold much more, with the ability to function as a completely autonomous contract. Put simply, instead of sending money to a specified account, Ether can be used to create a contract that completes as soon as conditions are met. This contract is verified, validated and put on the Ethereum blockchain, not moving until all terms have been met and the contract is complete.

What about mining?

Bitcoin mining requires the use of specialized hardware and, for a single user, is not likely to be profitable given the cost of the equipment and the energy required to carry out the mining. With Ethereum, however, a different system is in place, favoring those users with home computers rather than expensive gear that goes out of date very quickly. This is to encourage a much stronger network and more independent miners. That said, like Bitcoin, investment is required to earn money from Ethereum, just not as much as Bitcoin requires.

In both Ethereum and Bitcoin, miners make use of the computer power to solve the problems, known as 'proof of work' problems, resulting in the block of information being added to the blockchain. Both sets of miners are rewarded for mining each block and are paid in either Bitcoin or Ether.

Because the Bitcoin blockchain has a limited block size, each transfer can take an hour or more to be confirmed while transactions on Ethereum take, on average, about three minutes. The transaction fee that is paid to the miners has another use in Ethereum – it stops users from carrying out spam or other attacks against smart contracts and this is because of the high cost of large-volume transactions. Transaction fees on both are kept to a minimum.

Bitcoin mining for profit and investment is an extremely competitive field and in order to do so you have to follow some steps to ensure you can mine safely and profitably.

If you are a professional coder and have experience Linux or Ubuntu, then you may feel that your mining experience may be enhanced by using an established platform such as Genesis. Genesis mining is one of the leading cloud mining companies and provides the best option for smart ways to invest.

Join the team of experts and take advantage of the bitcoin mining algorithm that has been designed to provide rentals that can be used to mine in an efficient and reliable way.

Chances are you are more interested in a way for the individual with limited experience to enter the field of bitcoin mining.

It has to be pointed out that in the past mining could be done with an ordinary computer, but as the niche has become so competitive you will need to use ASIC miners, that's application specific integrated circuit to you and me, in order to mine successfully. Details of how you can obtain this hardware are available on the internet and you should be able to pick up what you need.

Firstly, we must ascertain if the process of bitcoin mining is even capable of producing a profit when applied to your circumstances. This can be worked out with a bitcoin mining calculator.

Once you have your mining calculator on your screen you will need to enter your mining hardware hash rate in GH/s, your power wattage and the cost of your electricity in dollars per Kw per hour. The calculator will automatically insert the level of difficulty, block reward and current bitcoin price.

Once the data has been entered you will receive a number of sets of figures. The calculations will be as follows

1. How many days it will take to generate one block of BTC with solo mining

2. How many days to generate a single bitcoin

3. How many days will it take to not see a loss

It is worth noting that all of these figures can vary greatly depending on exchange rates and sometimes just old-fashioned luck! These figures should also be taken as a guideline and should not be used to invest money. Any money used to invest in mining must be classed as "spare cash" due to the uncertainty and various variables that applies to the process.

You have now done your calculations and have decided you want to take this route. Time to choose your miner. There is plenty of material in the form of hardware reviews that can be used to help you make an informed choice.

Before we go any further a bitcoin wallet is needed, a fairly straightforward process. If you visit Bitcoin's site there are a host of alternative to choose from. In order to use your wallet for mining you will need to know your public address and not your private key.

Now we need to find a mining pool. It is not advised to mine individually as it is very unlikely that you will come across a bitcoin block and since that is how the currency is awarded, usually in a block of 12.5 at a time you will have more success when working as a group.

Choosing your pool is a very important part of the process. Below are the considerations that you must consider when choosing your pool.

1. Pool fee: Many consider this to be the main consideration when choosing your pool. Normally the fees range from 0% to 4% and the standard fee is generally 1%. If you find a pool that has the same

features as another but a lower fee then choose that one but keep an eye on the fee structure.

    a. It is also possible to find a pool that has a 0% fee, unusual but not unheard of. This would normally indicate a new pool that is looking to attract customers. Again, keep an eye on fee structures.

2. Payment system: General rule of thumb is determined by risk. If the pool operator is assuming the risk then it follows that they will pay a lower rate than a pool in which the miners assume the risk. This can also affect fee structure. Your first decision is to either accept a greater percentage of risk, pay less fees but accept that you may create less income. Alternatively, you could join a pool that guarantees a lower rate of profit but the pool operator guarantees payment for every proof of work.

3. Minimum payout: When choosing a pool, you will need to check out the payout period, the minimum payout and who is responsible for transaction fees. By

determining if it is the pool or the user who pays fees you can make informed choices.

4. Currency: Choosing the mining currency you wish to mine is a consideration you will need to address. Currently there are a number of alternatives. If you want to mix it up a little the multi-pool option may appeal to you. These allow mining of several crypto currencies at any time and can convert your profits into BTC once you decide to withdraw funds.

5. Geography: Always check your pool has servers in your country, or at least your continent! If they do check the URL for the servers and choose the one that allows you to mine more efficiently.

You will now need to get a mining program for your computer. If you have chosen a pool that already uses software like BitMinter then you are good to go. If, however the pool you have joined does not have its own software then you will need to choose your own.

Compare different mining software by checking the internet, two of the most popular programs are BFG miner and 50Miner.

All ready to go mining? Then let's begin! Connect your miner to the power and then attach it to your computer with a USB lead. Once you have opened up your mining software you will need to join your pool and enter your user name and password.

Once this is done you will begin mining for bitcoins, or your other chosen cryptocurrencies.

The actual process of mining is essentially releasing blocks of BTC by solving complex mathematical problems and algorithms. While there are millions of these equations surrounding each block of BTC not all of the equations have to be solved to release the block. This is where "chance" comes into play. You could unlock a block of BTC on the first, the hundredth or the millionth time you solve a problem.

The key is to find the winning equation that releases the block. How fast the problems are solved is determined by the speed and power of the computer solving it.

As a user, you are simply telling your computer that you want to mine, that is what the mining software is for, and at any one time there are tens of thousands of computers working on each equation at the same time and looking to release the same block of BTC. Therefore, it is suggested that you join a mining pool as opposed to working alone.

There has been four generations of mining hardware and modern miners are most likely to have dedicated mining rigs that are solely for the purpose of mining bitcoin.

Will there be a future without bitcoin mining? Simple answer- yes there will. It is believed that the final bitcoin will be produced by 2140 and as the final blocks are released there will be no more to reveal. Until then the number of people trying to mine currency grows every day and the chances of making a profit by this method becomes more difficult but that is the chance you take.

Bitcoin mining is a gamble, you will need to weigh up the pros and cons, examine the startup costs and decide if this is the route you want to take. If it is then happy mining and may your hard work bring you profit!!

Not your thing? Maybe you will be content simply buying currency and waiting for the price to rise. Whatever you decide then make sure you check out all information thoroughly.

Value and Decentralization

Both currencies are decentralized but Ethereum encourages users to mine with consumer graphic cards to prevent 51% attacks and collusion. The blockchain nodes for Bitcoin are grouped into pools and some of these pools control a high percentage of all the blocks that are mined. This leads to a higher risk of collusion.

Proof-of-work was the first solution that came out to protect the security of the blockchain. Ethereum developers have come up with a new way, one that increases decentralization even further and results in a lower cost with regards to computer

power. It's called a Proof-of-Stake system and it takes the place of mining with a system of staking the currency on whether or block can or should be put onto the blockchain.

Both Bitcoin and Ethereum are, by far the biggest cryptocurrencies on the market but, despite the volatility of both, Bitcoin has managed to keep its lead by a nose, as well as being the highest value cryptocurrency available right now. But what about other cryptocurrencies? How do they compare to Ethereum?

Ethereum vs Litecoin

Up until just recently, Litecoin was second to Bitcoin until it was firmly displaced by Ethereum. Comparing the two is like comparing a carrot with a beetroot. They may both be vegetables but that is where the similarity ends. Litecoin was originally released in 2011, as a way of overcoming challenges in Bitcoin mining. Litecoin mining times were shorter and where Bitcoin has a limit of 21 million coins, Litecoin went above and beyond this, aiming for a cap at 84 million tokens.

In terms of similarity, Ethereum and Litecoin are miles apart. Where Litecoin attempted to take over from Bitcoin, so Ethereum was slated to topple Litecoin, being released for a much bigger purpose than just mining and creating coins for transactions. Ether, the Ethereum currency, is created mainly to facilitate an exchange of value for services that are carried out on the platform. This platform is an immense decentralized computer powered by millions of other computers like the Bitcoin blockchain is. The core development team behind Ethereum have taken the necessary steps to stop the platform from being misused, purely for creating currency hand over fist, like they do on Litecoin and Bitcoin.

Litecoin also uses the Proof-of Work mining system that Bitcoin uses, again, different to the Proof-of-Stake algorithm used by Ethereum miners. It is this system that stops monopolization of the platform, as has happened with other cryptocurrencies – we have seen occurrences of both Litecoin and Bitcoin mining being taken over by large organizations with the money to purchase the most expensive equipment and fill up entire warehouses with it, effectively stopping the at-home miner from being able to compete. Proof-of-Stake makes it possible for everyone to be equal and it places a limit

on what functions may be performed on the Ethereum platform, simply through how much Ether each user possesses.

In short, Ethereum is a computational platform where Bitcoin and Litecoin are transactional systems. The currency is Ether and this is required for users to use any of the memory and processing power provided by the Ethereum protocol. Those who contribute get a reward of Ether and they can use this to build and host applications or trade it in for another type of cryptocurrency.

Litecoin, like Bitcoin, is a monetary platform, faster than Bitcoin and a good deal more efficient but, like Bitcoin, it has become a platform for those with the ability to invest serious money in mining, locking out the average user. It is highly unlikely that Litecoin will ever take back its crown as the second cryptocurrency and may even end up falling further as Ethereum continues to rise through the ranks.

Chapter 3: Real World Use of Ethereum

2016 proved to be very productive in terms of blockchain technology research and interest in it has resulted in several applications in industries across the world already. However, the blockchain isn't all that is turning heads.

Ethereum has introduced the smart contract, allowing for the automation of tasks that would normally require the intervention of third-parties thus promoting fewer oversight issues and less reliance on trust agents. It is the smart contract that has turned Ethereum into one of the most innovative platforms that could revolutionize different industries, in different ways.

Prediction and Financial Services Markets

In the near future, the financial services sector is going to expand rather quickly. Platforms, such as Branche, are planning to cause disruption to the industry through the introduction of Ethereum blockchain solutions for basic services like check cashing and Microcredit. As well as that, investors have also been given the opportunity to use a decentralized platform called ICONOMI, which is looking to give those investors the tools they need to return a decent profit in an economy that is decentralized.

A decentralized prediction market called Augur is a tool that predicts real-world events and it allows users to make a prediction on something that is happening right now and potentially make a profit if they are correct.

Real Estate

Several Ethereum projects are looking to cause disruption to the real estate market through the implementation of smart contracts. These contracts will cut down on the amount of friction caused by liens, payments and mortgage contracts. These smart contracts will also help to eliminate concerns about privacy between borrowers and lenders. One example of an Ethereum-based project is Rex MLS. This is an insurance platform that provides P2P access to all MLS information, including property listing and searching without the expense of hidden fees.

Identity and Privacy

Smart contracts will also be able to help streamline business processes by taking the place of traditional trust methods. Companies will be able to automate certain processes, like renewals, records release, and destruction. One project is called Trust Stamp and it uses data that is publicly available and social media to verify a user's identity, providing them with a unique trust score.

Another authentication and verification system is called Chainy, using timestamps to record things permanently onto the blockchain while Uport is an identity and key management system. Built with both developers and users in mind, it is made up of smart contracts and open-source libraries that allow used to own and control their identity, reputation, assets and online data.

Entertainment

The blockchain can mend issues with copyrights, tracking and payments, and there are several platforms already set up with the aim of decentralizing the music industry. They all make use of Ethereum and smart contracts to provide artists with complete control over their work by removing the likes of Spotify, SoundCloud and ReverbNation from the equation.

The gaming world has also expressed interest in Ethereum with several real-world games that provide users with a way of winning rewards. Gambling sites are jumping on the bandwagon, allowing users to deposit and claim their winnings in a fast and safe way. Not only will this cause disruption to the online gambling industry, it will also provide gamblers with safety and security from scams.

Lastly, there are the social media sites based on Ethereum, like Akasha. This site allows users to publish work, vote on other work and share it across the platform. It aims to be a decentralized version of WordPress but, unlike WordPress, Akasha provides rewards to those who come up with rich content though curator's rewards.

Smart Infrastructure

Ethereum has blasted into the smart infrastructure industry by facilitating the trading of, renting of and selling of energy and other peer-to-peer products. One Ethereum-based company called Slock.it is aiming to bring the blockchain and the Internet of Things together to help foster more P2P transactions. ElectricChain used Ethereum technology to hasten the speed at which solar energy takes off. They do this by going into partnership with other companies to provide incentives for the collection and use of solar energy.

LO3 Energy has just been awarded a patent that allows Ethereum-based energy trading. Together with Siemens, they came up with the Transactive Grid, a microgrid project in use in Brooklyn New York. The project is a P2P platform for energy trading that allows neighbors to buy and sell energy to and from each other.

The Health Industry

Ethereum has the potential to revolutionize health care systems across the world. Every hospital in the world will be able to store patient records, access them and share them when and where needed. This is one of the biggest factors in the development of new vaccinations for outbreaks of a viral nature or in the fight to prevent them from happening in the first place. You could, for example, go on holiday to Spain, pop in to see the doctor and then, when you return to

Manhattan, where you live, go to see your doctor there and both will have access to the exact same information about you.

It doesn't end there though. The recent craze in wearables is picking up steam and they are not going anywhere. Smartwatches record health data that could be shared with every single hospital in the world, allowing medical condition patterns to be spotted, such as strokes or heart attacks and you could be given a warning before it happens. In short, Ethereum could save your life.

Simpler Transactions

Right now, the entire economy of the world is based on transactions of one kind or another and these are about to be changed for good by Ethereum. Smart contracts will make it easy to exchange anything that is of value without any risk to either party. Instead of coming up with an old-fashioned paper contract, the whole thing will be done in computer code. Say, for example, you wanted to buy a photograph. Now, you would purchase it through a company like Shutterstock but, with a smart contract, you could set up a contract directly with the photographer. This can be done because of the built in IFTTT logic in Ethereum – If This Then That. The contract would state that, once the payment has been placed into an escrow service, the photograph will be sent. It could also say that, if the photo isn't sent, the payment will be returned to you.

Privacy from Third Parties

How many of you are aware that major search engines collect personal information from you and then sell it on to advertisers? And from that, they make a profit of billions every single year. By using the blockchain technology that Ethereum is based on, we can stop this from happening. Well, we can't stop the search engines from doing it but the technology can be used to log every single time those search engines use your information and data and will make those logs available publicly, for everyone to see. That way, the larger corporations will need to be a good deal more careful with the way they handle and use personal data if they don't want any damage done to their brand image.

Politics

Most people register to vote when the time comes around in their country, be it for local or national elections. However, not everyone places their vote because of a fear that their vote will not be counted or it will be altered in some way to favor a particular party. With Ethereum, voting and election fraud would be impossible. Because no one person has control of the network, every vote would be logged exactly as it was placed and everyone would be able to see it – they just wouldn't know who placed it. And that publicity means that no vote could be altered without everyone knowing about it, leading to a much fairer and more democratic system everywhere.

Self-Driving Cars

Some time ago, search engine giant Google announced plans to start mass-production of self-driving cars in 2020, hoping to revolutionize the way transport systems work. Ethereum has a vested interest in this because it is their technology that will back these vehicles up.

Self-drive cars are safer too because each communicates with the rest and that communication happens way faster than you or I could ever comprehend, let alone actually try.

Data Storage

The likes of Microsoft and Dropbox use server farms to store vast amounts of data. A server farm is a building full of these servers, each one full of information but they have one inherent problem – the company that owns them tends to concentrate a large proportion of capacity in one location. That opens the company up to a terrorist attack, natural disaster or some other way in which data can be stolen, lost or destroyed, resulting in substantial losses.

Decentralized storage facilities are the solution, facilities where information is not stored in one place; it is stored on millions of computers spread across the world. So far, this hasn't been possible because to the huge challenge involved in building the networks that could connect every server in safety and with fast rates of data transfer. The solution is likely to be Ethereum because the blockchain technology is designed to encrypt information and transfer data very quickly between all the servers

Prediction: Blokchain Changing The World In Many Ways

Below are examples of how blockchain technology through the use of **Etherum** applications will revolutionalized the world we live in for years to come!

Banks - Blockhain technology will enable almost everyone around the world, even people living in third world countries to have the means of financial access via bitcoin (BTC). -BTC uses fundamental blockchain technology to function.

Cyber Security - Although blockchain is accessible to the public it uses complex math and cryptography to enhance security, thus making it extremely difficult for anyone to hack and tamper with it.

Supply Chain Management - All transactions are permanently recorded in sequential order from point of begging to end, and constantly monitored through general consensus among the blockchain network for accuracy and authenticity purposes.- Increasing efficiency, reducing errors and time delays.

Insurance - Insurance is based on the principal of trust management, blockchain can be used to accurately verify data, such as insured person's identity, residence, etc. The chances for fraud is extremely slim as you know blockchain has state of the art advanced security measures.

Transportation -   We've all heard of Uber? Well now blockchain is looking to create decentralized peer to peer ride sharing apps, ways for car owners and users to establish terms and conditions of transportation without third party intermediaries (Uber).

Charity - Common issues with charities are corruption and inefficiencies. Blockchain technology will ensure transparent record keeping and create a permanent sequential, tamper resistant record to track, so there are no chances of money scandals or frauds we always hear about in the news. Ensuring only the intended recipient receives the funds.

Voting - Voting scandals and rigging can happen anywhere in the world, and even here in the west we are not immune to scandals, remember the 2016 US election? It's not the first time political parties have been accused for rigging results. Blockchain technology can be utilized for voter registration and identity confirmation , and also electronic vote counting would ensure only legitimate votes are counted.

No votes could be taken away or added, thus creating an indisputable publically accessible ledger. How's that for democracy?

Governments -   Government system are often slow, ambiguous and extremely frustrating. Implementing blockchain based systems will decrease bureaucracy, increase efficiency and uphold transparency.

Health Care - Secure storage platforms for information utilizing blockchain technology will enhance security and prevent hacking. Safely storing data such as medical records and sharing it only with the intended recipient. Improving data security and possibly even speed up diagnosis.

Energy Management - This has been a centralized monopoly for the longest time. But with blockchain technology you would be able to buy forms of energy, ie : electricity in a peer to peer fashion, thus electricity producers and users could buy directly from each other on a decentralized system. Currently we have to use trusted private intermediaries.

Online Music - Blockchain technology is working on a way to pay musicians and artists directly, instead of forfeiting large chunks of royalties to platforms or record labels. Artists/musicians would be able to keep more of the their profits!

Retail - Connecting buyers and sellers without additional fees. Exchanging in commerce without middlemen or intermediaries. In this case blockchain technology would use smart contract systems, and built in reputation management systems.

Real Estate - Eliminate the archaic paper based record keeping system, fraud, and uphold transparency. Blockchain would ensure ownership, accuracy, and even transferring property deeds.

Crowd Funding - A lot of companies use crowd funding platforms, however often times these platforms charge high fees. Blockchain could eliminate these fees by implementing smart contracts and online reputation based systems. New projects would release funds by generating their own "tokens" that have an associated value, and later be exchanged for products, services or cash.

Chapter 4: Investing in Ethereum

If you were looking to invest in an industry that shows a fast growth, there is a good chance that you would be looking at something in the tech sector or even marijuana stocks but, if you want something that has an accumulative return there your absolute best bet is Ethereum. Since 2017 started, despite a sudden drop in price, Ethereum's value has gone up by more than 2500% year to date. The S&P 500, by comparison, took almost 40 years to achieve those heady heights. There are a few ways to invest in Ethereum and we're going to talk about them here. Incidentally, one of the easiest ways is to purchase Bitcoin first and then use that to purchase Ether.

How Do I Buy Ether?

If you want to purchase Ether, the Ethereum currency, you will need to make use of an exchange. There are some exchanges that will store your keys for you, privately, and this makes it very easy to buy and sell but you do lose on the security aspect. There is also the issue of having a third-party looking after your information for you and that is not the idea of a decentralized system. If that exchange was hacked, and it has happened, your keys also get hacked and your access to your Ether is gone forever. The best alternative is to store your own keys offline or by using hardware – the most secure method but also the most difficult. You would need to be sure that your hardware never got corrupted or destroyed or you never lost the piece of paper that your keys get printed onto. Does it not also strike you as being just a little ironic that, to store your keys for a digital online currency, you need to use paper? More about storage later

What is an ICO?

An ICO is an Initial Coin Offering and it is a way of buying tokens in a specific company. In return, normally you will get some voting rights in the management of the company or, in some cases, a share of the profits. All of this is managed by way of the smart contracts we talked about earlier.

So how do you buy Ether?

The Easy Way – A Card Purchase

If this is your first time investing in a cryptocurrency, the best and easiest way is to go through CoinBase. They allow you to purchase and sell Ether using a credit card and they take away the need to get an exchange involved.

CoinBase is one of the best respected, the easiest to use and the most trustworthy way to purchase cryptocurrencies and they offer a decent desktop interface and a great mobile app. You can purchase any amount of Ether from $10 right up to $1000 in any coin. However, because they are one of the most popular, new registrations on CoinBase are reportedly being held up because of the increased demand, especially during peak times. These issues should be cleared fairly soon but, in the meantime, there are other ways to buy.

Cex.io

This is a full exchange, offering users the opportunity to purchase Ether using a credit card in USD, GBP or Euros. It is recommended that you sign up to both CoinBase and CEX as you will stand a chance of getting access when it is busy – especially if CoinBase goes down. This is one of the friendliest of all the main exchanges, offering a well-designed user-friendly interface.

BitPanda

BitPanda is primarily focused on the European market and is based in Austria. This exchange allows you to use SEPA, Skrill, and Visa to purchase Ether. Again, it has a very friendly user interface and also allows you, should you also purchase Bitcoins, to transfer them into vouchers for Amazon DE. This is a highly recommended exchange for anyone based in Austria or Germany.

Coinmama

Coinmama has only recently expanded into the Ether market and, right now you can only make your purchase using Euros or USD. However, they do accept all major credit

and debit cards for payment. The biggest benefit to using Coinmama is that, as soon as you have bought Ether, it is transferred directly to your wallet – more about those later – as opposed to some exchanges that hold your coins. With Coinmama, you have total control and have the ability to direct them to your exchange address or you can transfer them into another type of altcoin.

The Slightly Harder Way – Through an Exchange

The exchanges in this section may take longer for you to understand how they work and how to navigate their user-interface. However, often the fees are much lower and you get more features to play with. If you are looking for a more serious investment option, these are the better ones to get involved with.

It is also worth noting that withdrawals and deposits to these exchanges tend to be easier and that is a critical point – when you make a purchase through an exchange unless you are intending to sell it immediately, remove it to a wallet. If you don't and the exchange gets hit by a hacker you may lose all your Ether in one fell swoop. There is also the chance of a service outage on any exchange.

The downside is that not all of them make it easy to pay using Euros, GBP or USD and you may incur quite high bank fees if they do. This is only cost effective if you are buying a decent amount but it is always worth checking because you may not always be able to pay by card.

One of the best recommendations is to register with several exchanges – you don't need to make a purchase on each of them right away. It can take several days for account verification to be completed so you need to have them ready in case you need access. Not only that, prices can vary from exchange to exchange and you want the best price you can possibly get.

The best full exchanges to look at are:

- Poloniex
- Kraken
- Gemini

Other Services

eToro

This is a social trading platform that makes decisions that are based on social investment. Your investment will be based on the collation of actions by many and it offers a nice simple interface to help you make your investment.

eToro allows you to trade on an ETH/USD exchange, most probably the easiest way to get some exposure to the currency without the need to go too much into technical set ups. It is regulated by the UK FCA and is thought to be one of the safest methods of trading across a wide variety of markets.

A Copy Fund has recently been introduced by eToro, allowing you easier exposure to digital currencies and this gives you an easier way of making a mainstream investment without the need to monitor and manage your coins yourself.

It is important for you to understand that you will not own the coins through eToro; instead, you are making an investment in a price-tracking fund so make sure you only invest an amount that you can comfortably afford to lose.

How to Store Your Ether

You have purchased your Ether so what do you do now? Leave it where it is? Hope that the value is going to shoot up? Certainly, there is every chance that can happen but, similarly, there is also every chance it could plummet and the worst thing you could do is leave your currency sitting on the exchange while you wait for it to go up again. Not every exchange is up and running all the time and the only time that you will be able to access your Ether is when it is. That restricts your access. One of the most common

reasons for a service to go down, particularly in the case of CoinBase, is high demand or server problems and these are common.

So, the best thing you can do is store your Ether in a wallet and these come in several formats:

- Digital – stored on your mobile device or computer
- Paper – an archived print of you details
- Hardware – USB sticks that retain your keys and can only be accessed through a code. This is the most secure method

There are lots of arguments that go in favor of or against these wallets and each has its own benefits. The most crucial factor is that you, and you alone, maintain sufficient security on your wallet to keep your coins safe. If you lose your information or your wallet is compromised, you could lose everything. These are the most common wallets used for the storage of Ether:

A word of warning first – never lose your wallet password. If you do or you can't remember it you cannot access your wallet and there is no way to reset your password.

- **Jaxx**

Jaxx will run on a mobile, a desktop, and a browser and has support for many altcoins, including Ether, Bitcoin and Litecoin. It is dead simple to set up and very easy to use.

- **Mist**

Mist wallet is linked directly to the official website for Ethereum but it is a little on the slow side and can be very technical, not always suited for beginners.

- **My Ether Wallet (MEW)**

MEW is by far the best and most popular of all the Ether wallets. You do not need to sign up for it and set up is dead simple. There is plenty of help available for inexperienced users and experienced ones. The wallet is based on a local storage system and the password is the single most important bit of information that you will have.

MEW also provides support for sending Ether using a hardware wallet or you can generate a paper wallet, keeping your currency offline completely.

Hardware Wallets

Hardware wallets are very high tech, long term and incredibly secure forms of storage. Prices start at about 80 euros for anything decent so if you don't intend to spend that much on your Ether investment it may not be worth using one. The two most popular hardware wallets are Trezor and Ledger Nano S. Both do have relatively long waiting lists though so if you really want one, get your name down and then use one of the other wallets while you wait – and be patient!

Who is investing in Ethereum?

Although Ethereum can be seen as the child of Bitcoin, when it comes to future promise, it has shot past its predecessor, leaving it in the dust. There is one thing that sets Ethereum and Bitcoin worlds apart and that is the support that the former is receiving from both the technological and financial communities. Companies are beginning to realize the sheer power that blockchain technology provides in terms of efficiency and security and they want in.

Microsoft and JP Morgan are just two huge names that have pledged to support Ethereum's development by forming the Enterprise Ethereum Alliance, the purpose of which is to make sure that Ethereum's potential is fully realized across all industries. Companies that have joined the Alliance are working hard to ensure that a standard and open-source version of the platform is created, providing a blueprint of sorts for all future adaptations. JP Morgan is also working on its own Ethereum-based system of seamless fund transfers between its own branches across the world.

Although there are no small number of organizations that have invested in the leverage of Ethereum to act as a base for all privatized versions, one day, the goal they wish to attain is that every institution's private network will connect to the global blockchain, establishing a brand-new benchmark for transactions of information.

Other companies that have invested in Ethereum include:

- KYC-Chain – providing businesses with a safe way to attract new customers, using simple processes of identification and Know-Your-Customer. Customers are encouraged to manage their identities themselves, and only to share what information is necessary as and when needed.
- Colony – leveraging the Ethereum blockchains to drive organizations that are decentralized. It removes the traditional hierarchy of the organization and puts in place a simpler management of the distributed workforce. People are encouraged to invest expertise, time, ideas and feedback for global Ethereum projects. Based on an assessment system, users are given Ether tokens as rewards for completing tasks.

To list every company that has invested in Ethereum would take forever; suffice it to say that these are the tip of a very large iceberg.

Chapter 5: How Mining Works

Cryptocurrency mining is incredibly intensive work in terms of the processing power and the time that it takes. It is the participation in the distributed consensus network with the miner being rewarded in Ether tokens for coming up with solutions to the increasingly difficult math problems. Mining is done by pairing mining applications up with specific computer hardware.

All cryptocurrency transaction information must be embedded into a data block, with each block being lined through hash functions to the next and the previous block, hence the name, blockchain. Each block must be analyzed quickly to make sure that the platform runs smoothly but the developers of the Ethereum blockchain cannot do this alone – this is where the miners come in.

Miners are investors that give time space on their computer and energy to sort the blocks. When they come up with the right hash to solve the block, they submit their solution to the issues. Once it has been verified, the miner is given a reward, made up of a portion of the transaction they verified along with digital coins. The result of this is the Proof-of-Work system although Ethereum is switching over to a Proof of Stake System.

The only way, like Bitcoin, that Ethereum can be produced or created is through mining. However, with Ethereum, mining is doing more than just increasing the number of Ether in circulation – it is also used to secure the network as it works on the blocks in the blockchain. This process is essential to Ethereum because Ether is the fuel that keeps the platform running smoothly. One way of looking at it is that is a kind of incentive for developers to come up with fantastic applications. The supply of Ether is not infinite. Although there is no hard cap on it, it is limited to 25% of the initial issue at the presale, around 18 million Ether, every year.

For each block of Ether transactions to be validated in consensus, it must have the proof of work that proves the difficulty of it. Esthash is the name of the validation algorithm used and it is based on identification of the nonce input compared to the result in a way that it is lower than the initial threshold that was determined by the difficulty level. If all the outputs are uniformly distributed, the rewards are distributed on the time taken to find the nonce and that will depend on the difficulty of the block. In a case such as this, a miner can control the time needed to find the new bloc by manipulating the difficulty level.

Unlike Bitcoin, which is now too expensive and difficult, Ether can comfortably be mined from your own home. You will need to have knowledge of script writing and of the command prompt but it is relatively easy and very exciting once the process has been broken down into more manageable steps. Before you learn those steps, you need to understand the basics behind Ethereum mining.

The Basics

The first thing you need to understand is that mining takes a lot of power. However, provided your mining is done efficiently, you can generate income through the sale of the Ether. You can download a mining calculator from the internet which will give you some idea of what your profit will be.

You can use your home computer for Ethereum mining, unlike Bitcoin that requires expensive specialized hardware. The only caveats are that your graphic card must be a good one with a minimum of 2 GB RAM. Forget about CPU mining; it will just leave you frustrated, so much so that we are not even going to discuss it. GPU mining is far more efficient and at least 200 times faster than CPUs for mining purposes. If you have a Nvidia card, consider swapping it out for a decent AMD card as they are much better. You will also need at least 30 GB of free space on your computer – this is for the software you will need and to store the blockchain. Don't forget, the blockchain is constantly growing with each transaction that is added to it and if you can't store it, you can't mine.

The Procedure for Ethereum Mining

Follow these steps exactly for true mining success:

Step 1 - Download Geth. This is an application that serves as the communication hub, providing you with a link to the Ethereum platform while, at the same time, ensuring your setup is coordinated – that includes all your hardware and software. Geth will also provide you with reports on a development that you need to take action on.

Step 2 – Because Geth is in zipped file format, you will need to unzip it and extract the contents. Then you can transfer the Geth file to your hard drive. Most people stick to using C: but you can use a partition on your drive if you want.

Step 3 – To execute the application, you will need to use the command prompt. If you are using Windows, simply click on the search bar and type in CMD. Click on Command Prompt from the list of results.

Step 4 – The username placeholder on your computer is C:\Users\Username> and this provides the name given to your computer. It is the display that you will usually see in the command terminal. Your next step is to find Geth s, at the command prompt, type in cd/ and press the Enter button on your keyboard. This is a command that changes the directory and you should now see highlighted on the screen C:\> You are now in the C: drive.

Step 5 – Next comes account creation. To call Geth, at the command prompt, type in geth account new and press enter. You should now see C:\>geth account new at the command prompt.

Step 6 – Now you need to set up a password. Take care over this; make it a strong password and type it in carefully – you must remember this password! Press enter and your account with geth has been created.

Step 7 – Before you can do anything geth must link up to the network so, at the command prompt, type in geth -rpc and press enter. The Ethereum blockchain will begin to download and will synchronize with the global network. This is not a quick job and much will depend on how large the blockchain is and your computer and network speed. Do not do anything else until this step is complete.

Step 8 – Next, you must download the mining software. This will help your GPU to run the necessary hash algorithm. One of the better choices is Ethminer so find it on the internet and download it, then install it on your computer.

Step 9: Now change your directory again at the command prompt – see step 4 for instructions. Open a new command terminal by right-clicking the open one and selecting terminal from the popup menu

Step 10 – In this new window, type in cd prog and then press the tab key. You should now see C:\>cd prog on your terminal screen. Press the tab key again and you will see C:\>

cd "Program Files:' press the enter key again and you will see displayed C:\Program Files>

Step 11 – To get into the mining software folder, at the prompt, type in cd cpp and the press the tab key and the enter key. Press the tab key again and you should see C:\Prgram Files\cpp-ethereum on the display

Step 12 – To begin GPU mining, type in ethminer -G and press the enter key. The mining process will begin after the Directed Acrylic Graph (DAG) is built. This is a very large file that is stored on your GPU RAM for making it ASIC resistant. ASIC stands for Application Specific Integrated Circuits. Do make sure you have enough space on your hard drive before you do this.

Step 13 – If you want to, at this stage, you could have a go at CPU mining. All you need to do is type ETHMINER at the command prompt and then press the enter key. Again, the DAG will need to be built, after which Geth will begin communicating with Ethminer.

The Future of Ethereum Mining

Right now, Ethereum is using a Proof-Of-Work algorithm, the backbone of Bitcoin mining. Proof-of-Work is referring to finding solutions to complicated math equations, a fundamental requirement for any miner to get their block added to the blockchain. However, because of the sheer amount of energy it takes, this system has been pulled apart and Ethereum came up with another way. Using the Dagger Hashimoto algorithm, they have found a way that allows the home computer to mine relatively easily, without the added cost.

Also, they are planning to replace this system with a Proof of Stake System. This will remove the whole concept of mining and the new system will be powered by a consensus algorithm. Because the network is a string of computer-maintained connections, the profit that can be gained from mining Ether is somewhat surreal. Many miners are of the opinion that mining will come to a stop altogether when the new system comes into place – whether it will or not, only time will tell.

Chapter 6: What Does the Future Hold for Ethereum?

Right now, Ethereum is in an interesting place. Having fought through several battles, such as the DAO attack and the hard fork that followed, it has come through relatively unscathed. Now, it can expand and become what it was intended to be – a truly unique platform that is set to cause a huge disruption in industries the world over.

Ethereum is undergoing constant development and change and one of the biggest changes to date is the change over from Proof-of-Work to Proof-of-Stake. This is going to turn mining into a virtual process; instead of miners, there will be validators, who will be required to provide a certain amount of their Ether as a stake. Blocks are validated through the placement of a bet and the reward you get if the block is placed is in proportion to your initial investment. If your bet goes on a malicious block or the wrong block, you lose your Ether.

The advantages of this system are what will shape the future of the Ethereum platform:

- Lower costs in terms of energy and money – right now, Bitcoin miners are spending an average of $50,000 per hour on energy - $1.2 million every day. The proof-of-stake algorithm will cut these costs off almost completely because it will be a virtual system

- No advantage for ASIC hardware – there will be no advantages for those who have better hardware because the system won't depend on it
- 52% attacks will be harder – these happen when one person or a group has more than 50% of the hashing power in their control. Proof-of-stake will negate this.
- No malicious validators – because validators have to lock up a certain amount of their own Ether in the blockchain they are not likely to add any malicious or wrong blocks – they would lose their stake
- Faster block creation – the entire process of creating the new blocks will become more efficient and faster

This will also ensure the blockchain is more scalable because it will be much faster and easier to check who has invested the biggest stake than it is to see who has the highest amount of hashing power. Coming to a consensus will be simpler and more efficient.

The Future of Proof-of-Stake

At this moment, Casper, the POS algorithm is getting ready to be implemented. To begin with, mining will continue as normal but every 100th block will be subject to a POS check. Eventually, most of the block creation process will move over to POS and the way they are going to do it is through an ice age. What this means is that mining will become much harder and this will cut the hash rate. In turn, this will cut the speed of the chain and the decentralized applications that run on it, thus forcing everyone onto the POS system.

This is not going to be hassle-free. One massive fear is that the miners may force a hard fork in the blockchain before this can happen and then carry on with the new chain, mining as they always have done. Considering we already had one hard fork, this could potentially mean three blockchains running side by side.

Right now, this is nothing more than speculation. Before we get that far, there are two more phases of Ethereum implantation to go, the phases are:

- Frontier – the version everyone got when they started
- Homestead – the current phase
- Metropolis – the next phase
- Serenity – the final phase

Metropolis is being implemented but before we can even begin to look at it, there are three terms that you need to become au fait with:

- Abstraction
- Zk-snarks
- Sharding

Abstraction

What this means is that any protocol or system can be used by anyone without a need to know all the ins and outs, all the technical details that go with it. For example, you don't need to be an engineer to use an iPhone; you just need to know what buttons to press. You don't need to know about the circuits that are activated when you tap on an app or even how that app was programmed.

Zk-Snarks

This stands for Zero-Knowledge Succinct Non-Interactive Argument of Knowledge. The system has its base in zero knowledge proofs and that works something like this – you have two separate parties – a prover and a verifier. The prover is able to prove to the verifier that they know a certain piece of information without actually revealing that information, thus aiding in privacy.

Sharding

Sharding means nothing more than breaking a massive database down into smaller shards. Each shard will have its own validators and this will help with scalability.

Metropolis

There are 4 main implementations in the Metropolis Phase:

- Implementation of several Ethereum Improvement Protocols – EIPs, which will work to make the Ethereum platform more robust
- Flexibility for smart contracts. They will have the ability to pay their fees without the need for external funding from users
- The first steps to abstraction – to make Ethereum more user-friendly to the masses. One possible

innovation may be that users will be allowed to pay their Ethereum transaction costs using another cryptocurrency other than Ether

- Zk-Snarks will be introduced

Serenity

Although the implementation of Serenity is some way off, it will be the final one, Ethereum as it should be. When Serenity is finally launched, this will be the result:

- More EIPS will be implemented
- Proof-of-Work will be gone and will be entirely replaced by Proof-of-Stake
- A total abstraction of the Ethereum platform
- Blockchain sharding will be implemented. This will ensure that the blockchain, all transactions, and all the decentralized applications that run on Ethereum will be able to run a great deal faster and block creation times will decrease exponentially. It is expected that the times will drop to below 4 seconds per block – compare that to the 10 to 20 minutes that Bitcoin blocks currently take.

The Future of Ethereum

With all of this, there is no doubt that Ethereum has an incredibly bright future. Ultimately, Ethereum has one aim – to "disappear" although not literally. The ultimate goal is for Ethereum to become omnipresent, running on everything without everyone being aware that they are working on or using an Ethereum-based system.

Summary

Etherum is the digital oil and framework. Etherum has several applications and is very versatile. Unlike bitcoin which is only really used as a form of currency in commerce. The best way to comprehend what Etherum is to use an anaology, earlier I called Etherum a digital oil and similar to petroleum it has various functions and uses. While bitcoins can be considered a one dimensional property that can only be used for one thing and that is a form of currency.

Remember in essence Etherum is basically a blockchain technology, however, the main difference is with Etherum you can actually build things, ie: bitcoins and other cryptocurrencies, additionally you can also build social networks, and decentralized information sources similar to wikipedia. The programming language in Etherum is like Java or CC+, meaning you can build almost anything!

So for example, if you wanted to build the next "Facebook" or another social media platform using Etherum it would be completely decentralized! That means there would be no third party intermediaries, no incorporation and no authoritative figure. Therefore, all users would be communicating directly, peer to peer, and all the data and information collected would belong to the users and not anyone else!

So think how this would translate into add campaigns and the such? Users would be directly paid, instead of money being funneled through third party intermediaries who take a cut or hold on to the funds. Incredibly enough this actually equates to you being a "shareholder" of the network technically speaking. Exciting right?

So whatever network or application you are engaging with, you'd automatically become a shareholder! Imagine a new application or platform just launched, and in order to utilize their services they hand out tokens as a means of purchasing services. Now if the application becomes popular and more people join all the first time user's tokens would rise in value as now there would be a demand for them, and thus creates a sort of shareholder paradigm.

In essence Etherum is a platform for decentralized applications. The future looks bright for Etherum, more and more people in society are realizing the true value this technology can bring. Microsoft and other giant corporations are heavily investing in Etherum as we speak. The potential is recognized and the future seems boundless. It's really important to understand the power of this amazing technology and it will transform the way the internet works. The basic architecture for the internet as we have it now is clients need to go through servers, for instance when I go to Facebook my browser is the client and needs to connect to the central Facebook server, and then all the communication goes through the centralized server. But, with a decentralized social network server all my messages will be sent directly to the users whom I want to talk with and not a central server.

This is incredible for the future! This could mean we could literally be reengineering the way communication occurs in cyberspace. What are your thoughts on Etherum? Will this technology revolutionize the world? Only time will tell.

Bonus Chapters

Bitcoin Expanded

Although the history of BTC is somewhat obscure the estranged man behind both the development of BTC and the initial stages of blockchain is Satoshi Nakamoto. This all started approximately in the year 2008. It is believed Mr. Nakamoto posses *1 million* BTC that have a cash value of **2.7 billion USD**!! (Present year 2017)

The group of people who assisted in the development of BTCs is still an enigma and there is a lot of mystery that shrouds this question even today, however we do know for certain that Mr. Nakamoto and his group of developers intended to have some sort of new electronic cash system implemented during economic crisis between the years 2007 - 2008. This was an extremely strategic and clever ploy trying to leverage the world's economic turmoil and capitalize on it by introducing a totally radical, new, unparalleled, and revolutionary currency.

This cryptocurrency would be the first ever intangible form of money that only exists in "cyberspace". BTC has its limits, and by that I mean it is a finite currency and capped at a maximum threshold of 21 million to be brought into existence. Meaning once that cap is reached no more BTC can ever be produced.

There is a lot of controversy surrounding the true identity of Mr. Satoshi Nakamoto or if this is even a real person. There are a lot of speculations ranging from being someone from "common wealth origins" to being a Japanese - American born systems engineer, I cannot give a definitive answer to this conjecture. But, what I can say is ever since the debut of BTC it has been continuously gaining upward momentum and shows no signs of slowing down and is currently worth *2739.26 USD* per BTC! That's right, $2739 USD for a single bitcoin! (current value estimated **July 2017**)

Obviously just like any market share value will fluctuate due to various factors in the free market. Therefore, you can expect big spikes and deep declines, but I can say BTC is most definitely a lucrative prospect and something worthwhile investing in. It is a currency that is here to stay for the foreseeable future and will continue to impact the lives of millions of people worldwide.

BTC has made more than a handful of people millionaires, including myself. How was this done? Simply put I zoned in on an opportunity, saw a trend and predicted the future based on past patterns. Not difficult at all right? Perhaps I used a bit of "chance" too, I was in the right place at the right time. In all honesty, when it comes to capitalizing on trends you must be able to discern, time, and take massive action towards it, and then you will be rewarded with fruition from the risk you took. Before BTC gained its high value, when youtube videos, blogs on BTC, and "How to do" books /articles weren't around, BTC's value was worth less than a fraction of its value today.

Me and many others purchased BTC when they were priced around $14 -$35 USD per BTC. As you can see the price has exponentially increased and those who invested early as always reap massive results! Now you're probably questioning is it too late to join in on the "BTC gold rush"? My answer is, NO. There is still a massive opportunity that exists to make a killing and capitalize on this BTC trend.

Historical Trends

Since the history of mankind technological advancements that spurred waves of monumental change shaped the world in which we live today, such as the renaissance, industrial age, etc. At any given period of time in history we see patterns, trends and paradigms that shape the world we live in today.

BTC will be the next BIG trend and will shift government policies, regulations, and legislation forever. Imagine a decentralized system with no authoritative institutions s in control, no detrimental government intervention, but only the will of the people manifested through an autonomous currency. Isn't this incredible?

Of course people will be skeptical at first, but as we look at history's historical trend we can see anytime massive change or revolution occurs it was always met with opposition, consisting of people who are skeptic about change. Anytime new knowledge or technology was implemented it was always mocked, ridiculed and even denied.

Please see below an excerpt from the book Blockchain Technology & Blueprint Ultimate Guide. You can see recent historical events that occurred that continue to change the world for the better in which we live today..

"We live in the digital age and it would only make sense that currency would eventually follow in the transition into the digital realm, ie: cryptocurrency. This is not merely speculation or abstract conjecture, but this is based on trends and a few facts. Let's take a look at some of the things we interface with on a daily basis that have also stepped into the world digitization."

Books - In the past libraries were the only source to get access to books and other information packages. But, now we have digital books (kindle, Kobo,etc).

Music/Podcasts - Before you had to buy records, tapes, and CDs to listen to your favorite artist. Now we have itunes and other platforms that allow you to instantly listen to music without having to go through the hassle of buying an actual physical product. Digital access to music eliminates the damaged merchandise factor, for example a scratch on a CD would render the music on it inaudible, meaning you would have to go buy another copy! With music being digital you eliminate such inconveniences.

Video Games - Synonymous to music this too has stepped into the digital era. Games use to be purchased on cartridges and most recently CDs, but now can all be downloaded at the touch of a button online for instant access.

Mail - Before the invention of the E-mail the vast majority of people in society solely relied on mail couriers (mail men/women) as a means of relaying communication. However, since the advent and successful launch of the E-mail people now communicate worldwide with lightning speed! Uninterrupted by time zones and other external factors.

Bill Payments - In the past the average person had to rely on cheques to get paid and to exchange large volumes of cash in any given transaction. Bills would have to be paid by cheque, and the period of waiting times were immensely long. But, now we have direct deposits (Electronic Wire Transfers) and other similar electronic deposits. We can even make bill payments and purchases directly from our smart phones!

As you can see the above historical trends, some more recent than others indicates quite a few things, 1. accessibility and autonomy is an increasing trend, and 2. Evolution is an inevitable variable and we must adapt accordingly. It's only a matter of time when currency also follows in the digital paradigm. After all this is the digital age, right?

Advantages:

Decentralized system - Nobody has ownership, no authoritative institutions have control, and governments cannot intervene.

Utilizes BlockChain technology - Because BTC uses blockchain technology it makes this cryptocurrency tamper resistant and extremely difficult for fraud and any other shady transactions unlikely.

Hyper Ledger - utilizes a ledger that records every single transaction that occurs. Which can be used to trace transaction with pinpoint accuracy from point of origin to finish.

Finite Currency - BTC is a finite currency and has a cap. Meaning unlike banks, you cannot print out new money on demand. (this is what causes inflation - money loses value)

***Accounts Cannot Be Frozen* -** It's a known fact that banks for whatever reasons, when they become suspicious of certain financial activity they have the right to either freeze your account or terminate it without any warning or legitimate reason. Don't believe me? Read the fine print the next time you sign up with whomever you decide bank with.

This has actually happened to a friend of mine before, he use to operate an event management company which was quite lucrative, and one time he was expecting a deposit of **250,000 USD** and even advised the branch manager at the time, but can you guess what happened? For whatever reason they still decided to flag his personal bank account and it was frozen for "further investigation" and there was absolutely nothing he could do about it.

He ran a legitimate business, and fortunately he did eventually get access to his bank account 2 weeks later, however imagine the amount stress and headaches he had to go through. He had to pay vendors, employees, and other expenses, yet he could not touch any of his money that he rightfully owned.

But with BTC accounts cannot be frozen. So if the same scenario went down with depositing BTC he would of had no hassle or any problems whatsoever.

No Prerequisites - Laws and regulations vary from country to country, however the fact is that banks have limits and arbitrary rules to control your money. With BTC all you.

Direct Person To Person Transfer- With BTC there are no intermediaries, clearing houses or middlemen you find with traditional banks. I personally like this approach a lot better as large volume transactions can be done with ease, fluidly and efficiently with no long waiting times. Money can be received instantly.

Transaction Fees Significantly Decreased - Let's face it banks are not looking for the best interest of the people. Expensive transaction and hidden fees is something we are all constantly bombarded with, and can be costly. But with BTC you will face significantly reduced fees compared to banks.

Disadvantages

No customer technical or customer support - Since BTC runs on a decentralized system, when you run into trouble perhaps your hard drives crashes, you lost your password or unique key code, the fact is you have nobody to turn to. Banks would have customer support.

Bitcoin Value Volatile - Simply put the value of BTC can be erratic, and if someone hypothetically came up with a better cryptocurrency with a greater algorithm what happens to BTC? The value would surely drop, and thus BTC can be considered unstable for this reason.

Negative perceptions - Ever since the rise of "silk road" a black market website selling illegal goods in exchange for BTC, bitcoins got quite a bad rep due to the fact it was used as a veil for criminals to conduct commerce under.

Banks Do Not Support Bitcoin - The fact is BTC threatens the very existence of financial institutions and they do not at all like the fact that BTC a decentralized system and currency exists. Banks have terminated many accounts of users who engaged in mixing BTC with their bank accounts.

No Physical Properties - BTC in reality has no actual value, but just like any fiat currency it is given value by us. Remember BTC is intangible, it's not like gold, silver or copper.

BTC is an electronic currency that is based on a unified maintained ledger. People transfer "bitcoin currency" by sending messages to the bitcoin network known as maintainers or "miners" who verify signatures in the form of complex math equations. Maintainers/miner do a general consensus to find out the accurate solution and verify the authenticity of the message from the account holder.

BTC in actual fact has no value, but achieves its value because we give it value just like any other fiat currency. BTC is a completely intangible substance unlike the physical currency we use today.

We must highlight an important aspect of BTC, and that's what happens if user error mistakes are made, such as hard drive crashes which stores your pertinent "key code information"? This will result in a permanent loss of BTC associated with the account holder's private key code.

Since its a decentralized system there is no technical support or bank teller assistance you can turn to, thus your BTCs are lost forever.

Conclusion

I want to thank you for taking the time to read my guide. I hope that you now have a better understanding of what Ethereum is all about and how you can make a profit from it by investing or mining.

Despite the fact that it is still not close to the value of Bitcoin, Ether has been on an impressive growth spurt just recently. Since it made its debut on the eToro platform in January 2017, impressive and incredibly gains have been registered, its value quadrupling almost overnight. Of course, some of that could be down to a decision made recently by the SEC to deny a Bitcoin-based ETF, perhaps causing some investors to turn to Ether instead.

Ether is a new currency, just a couple of years old and it still depends quite a lot on the sentiment that cryptocurrencies seem to generate, although this is dictated mostly by Bitcoin. The original cryptocurrency is firmly established as an asset for a large number of traders, especially with the large swings it presents almost daily. Bitcoin has also been showing impressive gains but, in terms of the future, Ethereum is fast catching up and is ready to take over.

Bitcoin may still be the benchmark for overall market sentiment but the recent decision from the SEC has pushed it away from the mainstream market and this could well be why Ether is now surging in value. It isn't that far out to assume that many traders in cryptocurrencies are now turning to Ether as a viable alternative and especially as it hasn't yet had to face this kind of media trial.

Not only that, Ether is firmly established in its own right and is prone to upset by factors that do not have anything to do with Bitcoin. Because Ether is based on the blockchain, there are several development tools that could use Ether as their currency and that means any change in the Ethereum platform could influence the currency.

Whenever a hard fork is reached, a programming change that makes the platform backwards incompatible, Ether may well be severely affected – these could be positive, perhaps better security or better accessibility, or they could be negative as in the case of the DAO hard fork, an act that left the door open for the theft of $50 million in Ether, effecting a 30% value drop in 24 hours. That hack has been sorted and the value has begun climbing steadily again.

We can't yet determine whether Ethereum is going to be the next Bitcoin but we do expect to see a sizeable fluctuation in Ether prices as the future unfolds. It has the potential to carry on climbing becoming a very serious rival to Bitcoin or it could plummet hard, leading to its eventual demise. If the price of Bitcoin drops substantially, it can also take Ethereum down with it.

That said, Bitcoin has done a lot of work in paving the way for Ethereum. The market is now more tolerant and accepts digital currencies. This could be the start of a new era in money and finance, a new era where the strongest currencies are digital.

Ethereum is an interesting prospect and is one to watch now and in the future. Do be aware of the risks of investing though – it carries the same risks that any investment does so never invest any more than you can afford to lose.